The Writings of Alexander of Lycopolis

The Writings of Alexander of Lycopolis

The Writings of Alexander of Lycopolis

© Lighthouse Publishing 2024

Written by: Alexander of Lycopolis (AD 301)
Translated by: Rev. James B.H. Howkins (1879)
Updated into Modern U.S English: A.M. Overett (b.1960)

All rights reserved. Without limiting the rights under copyright reserved above, no part of this publication may be reproduced, stored in a retrieval system, or transmitted, in any form or by any means (electronic, mechanical, photocopying, recording or otherwise), without the prior written permission of the copyright owner of this book.

Published by
Lighthouse Publishing
SAN 257-4330
228 Freedom Parkway
Hoschton, GA 30548
United States of America

www.lighthousechristianpublishing.com

Introductory Notice
to
Alexander, Bishop of Lycopolis.

[a.d. 301.] To the following account, translated from Galland, I prefix only the general date of Alexander's episcopate. He was succeeded in the bishopric of Lycopolis by the turbulent Meletius, of whose schism we need not say anything here. But his early relations with the heresy of Manes, and his subsequent orthodoxy (in all which he was a foreshadowing of Augustine), render his treatise on the Manichæan opinions especially valuable. Combefis conjectured that Alexander was called Λυκοπολίτης, as having been born at Lycus, a city of the Thebaid, and so by race an Egyptian, and to his opinion both Cave and Fabricius are inclined. But this conjecture is plainly uncertain, if we are to trust Photius, in his *Epitome De Manichæis*, which Montfaucon has edited. For in this work Photius, whilst speaking of the authors who wrote against those heretics, makes mention also of Alexander as bishop of the city of Lycus, ὅτε τῆς πόλεως Λύκων Ἀλέξανδρος τοὺς ἀρχιερατικοὺς νόμους ἐγκεχειρισμένος. So that it is no easy matter to state whether our author was called Λυκοπολίτης, because he was born either at Lycopolis in the Thebaid, or at another Lycopolis in Lower Egypt, which Stephanus places close to the sea in the Sebennytic nome, or whether he was not rather called Λυκοπολίτης, as having held the bishopric of Lycopolis. The unwonted manner of speaking employed by Photius need not delay the attention of anyone, when he makes Alexander to have been Archbishop of Lycopolis; for it is established that the Bishop of Alexandria alone was

Archbishop and Patriarch of the whole Egyptian diocese. Epiphanius certainly says, when speaking of Meletius, the schismatical Bishop of Lycopolis, ἐδόκει δὲ ὁ Μελήτιος τῶν κατὰ τὴν Αἴγυπτον προήκων, καὶ δευτερεύων τῷ Πετρῳ τῷ τῆς Ἀλεξανδρείας κατὰ τὴν ἀρχιεπισκοπήν. And to the same purpose he says elsewhere, Μελήτιος, ὁ τῆς Αἰγύπτου ἀπὸ Θηβαΐδος δοκῶν εἶναι καὶ αὐτὸς ἀρχιεπίσκοπος. But however these matters are understood, it is admitted that Alexander came just before Meletius in the See of Lycopolis, and we know that he occupied the episcopal chair of that city in the beginning of the fourth century, in which order Le Quien places him among the Lycopolitan prelates, on the authority of Photius.

In the time of Constantine, the Eastern and Western Empire were each divided into seven districts, called dioceses, which comprised about one hundred and eighteen provinces; each province contained several cities, each of which had a district attached to it. The ecclesiastical rulers of the dioceses were called patriarchs, exarchs, or archbishops, of whom there were fourteen; the rulers of the provinces were styled metropolitans, i.e., governors of the μητρόπολις or mother city, and those of each city and its districts were called bishops. So that the division which we now call a diocese, was in ancient times a union of dioceses, and a parish was a combination of modern parishes.

But however it be, whether Alexander was called Λυκοπολίτης from his birthplace, or from his episcopal See, this is certain and acknowledged, that he of good right claims for himself a place among ecclesiastical writers, for he has given us an elaborate treatise against the Manichæan tenets; and he is therefore styled by

Allatius *auctor eruditissimus et* φιλοσοφικώτατος, and his work *libellus aureus*. Allatius wrote out and brought to light two passages from it, while as yet it was lying hid in the libraries. From the inscription of the work, we learn that Alexander was first a pagan; and afterwards, having given up the religion of the Greeks, became an adherent of the Manichæan doctrines, which he says that he learnt from those who were on terms of familiar intercourse with the heresiarch, ἀπὸ τῶν γνωρίμων τοῦ ἀνδρός; so that he would seem to be not far wrong in his conjecture who would place our author at no very distant date from the times of Manes himself. From the errors of this sect he was divinely reclaimed, and, taking refuge in the Church, he exposed the scandals attaching to the heresiarch, and solidly refuted his unwholesome dogmas. From having been an adherent of the sect himself, he has given us more information concerning their tenets than it was in the power of others to give, and on that account his treatise seems to be held in much estimation.

Of the Manichæans.

Chapter I.—The Excellence of the Christian Philosophy; The Origin of Heresies Amongst Christians.

The philosophy of the Christians is termed simple. But it bestows very great attention to the formation of manners, enigmatically insinuating words of more certain truth respecting God; the principal of which, so far as any earnest serious purpose in those matters is concerned, all will have received when they assume an efficient cause, very noble and very ancient, as the originator of all things that have existence. For Christians leaving to ethical students matters more toilsome and difficult, as, for instance, what is virtue, moral and intellectual; and to those who employ their time in forming hypotheses respecting morals, and the passions and affections, without marking out any element by which each virtue is to be attained, and heaping up, as it were, at random precepts less subtle—the common people, hearing these, even as we learn by experience, make great progress in modesty, and a character of piety is imprinted on their manners, quickening the moral disposition which from such usages is formed, and leading them by degrees to the desire of what is honorable and good.

But this being divided into many questions by the number of those who come after, there arise many, just as is the case with those who are devoted to dialectics, some more skillful than others, and, so to speak, more sagacious in handling nice and subtle questions; so that now they come forward as parents and originators of sects and heresies. And by these the formation of morals is hindered and rendered obscure; for those do not attain unto certain verity of discourse who wish to become the heads of the sects, and the common people is to a greater degree excited to strife and contention. And there being no rule nor law by which a solution may be obtained of the things which are called in question, but, as in other matters, this ambitious rivalry running out into excess, there is nothing to which it does not cause damage and injury.

Chapter II.—The Age of Manichæus, or Manes; His First Disciples; The Two Principles; Manichæan Matter.

So in these matters also, whilst in novelty of opinion each endeavors to show himself first and superior, they brought this philosophy, which is simple, almost to a nullity. Such was he whom they call Manichæus, a Persian by race, my instructor in whose doctrine was one Papus by name, and after him Thomas, and some others followed them. They say that the man lived when Valerian was emperor, and that he served under Sapor, the king of the Persians, and having offended him in some way, was put to death. Some such report of his character and reputation has come to me from those who were intimately acquainted with him. He laid down two principles, God and Matter. God he called good, and matter he affirmed to be evil. But God excelled more in good than matter in evil. But he calls matter not that which Plato calls it, which becomes everything when it has received quality and figure, whence he terms it all-embracing—the mother and nurse of all things; nor what Aristotle calls an element, with which form and privation have to do, but something besides these. For the motion which in individual things is incomposite, this he calls matter. On the side of God are ranged powers, like handmaids, all good; and likewise, on the side of matter are ranged other powers, all evil. Moreover, the bright shining, the light, and the superior, all these are with God; while the obscure, and the darkness, and the inferior are with matter. God, too, has desires, but they are all good; and matter, likewise, which are all evil.

Chapter III.—The Fancies of Manichæus Concerning Matter.

It came to pass on a time that matter conceived a desire to attain to the superior region; and when it had arrived there, it admired the brightness and the light which was with God. And, indeed, it wished to seize on for itself the place of pre-eminence, and to remove God from His position. God, moreover, deliberated how to avenge Himself upon matter, but was destitute of the evil necessary to do so, for evil does not exist in the house and abode of God. He sent, therefore, the power which we call the soul into matter, to permeate it entirely. For it will be the death of matter, when at length hereafter this power is separated from it. So, therefore, by the providence of God, the soul was commingled with matter, an unlike thing with an unlike. Now by this commingling the soul has contracted evil, and labors under the same infirmity as matter. For, just as in a corrupted vessel, the contents are oftentimes vitiated in quality, so, also the soul that is in matter suffers some such change, and is deteriorated from its own nature so as to participate in the evil of matter. But God had compassion upon the soul, and sent forth another power, which we call *Demiurge*, that is, the Creator of all things; and when this power had arrived, and taken in hand the creation of the world, it separated from matter as much power as from the commingling had contracted no vice and stain, and hence the sun and moon were first formed; but that which had contracted some slight and moderate stain, this became the stars and the expanse of heaven. Of the matter from which the sun and the moon was separated, part was cast entirely out of the world, and is that fire in which, indeed, there is the power of burning, although in itself it is dark and void of light, being closely similar to night. But in the rest of the elements, both animal and vegetable, in those the divine power is unequally mingled. And therefore the world was made, and in it the sun and moon who preside over the birth and death of things, by separating the divine virtue from matter, and transmitting it to God.

Chapter IV.—The Moon's Increase and Wane; The Manichæan Trifling Respecting It; Their Dreams About Man and Christ; Their Foolish System of Abstinence.

He ordained this, forsooth, to supply to the *Demiurge*, or Creator, another power which might attract to the splendor of the sun; and the thing is manifest, as one might say, even to a blind person. For the moon in its increase receives the virtue which is separated from matter, and during the time of its augmentation comes forth full of it. But when it is full, in its wanings, it remits it to the sun, and the sun goes back to God. And when it has done this, it waits again to receive from another full moon a migration of the soul to itself, and receiving this in the same way, it suffers it to pass on to God. And this is its work continually, and in every age. And in the sun some such image is seen, as is the form of man. And matter ambitiously strove to make man from itself by mingling together all its virtue, so that it might have some portion of soul. But his form contributed much to man's obtaining a greater share, and one beyond all other animals, in the divine virtue. For he is the image of the divine virtue, but Christ is the intelligence. Who, when He had at length come from the superior region, dismissed a very great part of this virtue to God. And at length being crucified, in this way He furnished knowledge, and fitted the divine virtue to be crucified in matter. Because, therefore, it is the Divine will and decree that matter should perish, they abstain from those things which have life, and feed upon vegetables, and everything which is void of sense. They abstain also from marriage and the rites of Venus, and the procreation of children, that virtue may not strike its root deeper in matter by the succession of race; nor do they go abroad, seeking to purify themselves from the stain which virtue has contracted from its admixture with matter.

Chapter V.—The Worship of the Sun and Moon Under God; Support Sought for the Manichæans in the Grecian Fables; The Authority of the Scriptures and Faith Despised by the Manichæans.

These things are the principal of what they say and think. And they honor very especially the sun and moon, not as gods, but as the way by which it is possible to attain unto God. But when the divine virtue has been entirely separated off, they say that the exterior fire will fall, and burn up both itself and all else that is left of matter. Those of them who are better educated, and not unacquainted with Greek literature, instruct us from their own resources. From the ceremonies and mysteries, for instance: by Bacchus, who was cut out from the womb, is signified that the divine virtue is divided into matter by the Titans, as they say; from the poet's fable of the battle with the Giants, is indicated that not even they were ignorant of the rebellion of matter against God. I indeed will not deny, that these things are not sufficient to lead away the minds of those who receive words without examining them, since the deception caused by discourse of this sort has drawn over to itself some of those who have pursued the study of philosophy with me; but in what manner I should approach the thing to examine into it, I am at a loss indeed. For their hypotheses do not proceed by any legitimate method, so that one might institute an examination in accordance with these; neither are there any principles of demonstrations, so that we may see what follows on these; but theirs is the rare discovery of those who are simply said to philosophize. These men, taking to themselves the Old and New Scriptures, though they lay it down that these are divinely inspired, draw their own opinions from thence; and then only think they are refuted, when it happens that anything not in accordance with these is said or done by them. And what to those who philosophize after the manner of the Greeks, as respects principles of demonstration, are intermediate propositions; this, with them, is the voice of the prophets. But here, all these things being eliminated, and since those matters, which I before mentioned, are put forward without any demonstration, and since it is necessary to give an answer in a rational way, and not to put forward other things more plausible, and which might prove more enticing, my attempt is rather troublesome, and on this account the more arduous, because it is necessary to bring forward arguments of a varied nature. For the more accurate arguments will escape the observation of those who have been convinced beforehand by these men without proof, if, when it comes to persuasion, they fall into the same hands. For they imagine that they proceed from like sources. There is, therefore, need of much and great diligence, and truly of God, to be the guide of our argument.

Chapter VI.—The Two Principles of the Manichæans; Themselves Controverted; The Pythagorean Opinion Respecting First Principles; Good and Evil Contrary; The Victory on the Side of Good.

They lay down two principles, God and Matter. If he (Manes) separates that which comes into being from that which really exists, the supposition is not so faulty in this, that neither does matter create itself, nor does it admit two contrary qualities, in being both active and passive; nor, again, are other such theories proposed concerning the creative cause as it is not lawful to speak of. And yet God does not stand in need of matter in order to make things, since in His mind all things substantially exist, so far as the possibility of their coming into being is concerned. But if, as he seems rather to mean, the unordered motion of things really existent under Him is matter, first, then, he unconsciously sets up another creative cause (and yet an evil one), nor does he perceive what follows from this, namely, that if it is necessary that God and matter should be supposed, some other matter must be supposed to God; so that to each of the creative causes there should be the subject matter. Therefore, instead of two, he will be shown to give us four first principles. Wonderful, too, is the distinction. For if he thinks this to be God, which is good, and wishes to conceive of something opposite to Him, why does he not, as some of the Pythagoreans, set evil over against Him? It is more tolerable, indeed, that two principles should be spoken of by them, the good and the evil, and that these are continually striving, but the good prevails. For if the evil were to prevail, all things would perish. Wherefore matter, by itself, is neither body, nor is it exactly incorporeal, nor simply any particular thing; but it is something indefinite, which, by the addition of form, comes to be defined; as, for instance, fire is a pyramid, air an octahedron, water an eikosahedron, and earth a cube; how, then, is matter the unordered motion of the elements? By itself, indeed, it does not subsist, for if it is motion, it is in that which is moved; but matter does not seem to be of such a nature, but rather the first subject, and unorganized, from which other things proceed. Since, therefore, matter is unordered motion, was it always conjoined with that which is moved, or was it ever separate from it? For, if it were ever by itself, it would not be in existence; for there is no motion without something moved. But if it was always in that which is moved, then, again, there will be two principles—that which moves, and that which is moved. To which of these two, then, will it be granted that it subsists as a primary cause along with God?

Chapter VII.—Motion Vindicated from the Charge of Irregularity; Circular; Straight; Of Generation and Corruption; Of Alteration, and Quality Affecting Sense.

There is added to the discourse an appendix quite foreign to it. For you may reasonably speak of motion not existing. And what, also, is the matter of motion? Is it straight or circular? Or does it take place by a process of change, or by a process of generation and corruption? The circular motion, indeed, is so orderly and composite, that it is ascribed to the order of all created things; nor does this, in the Manichæan system, appear worthy to be impugned, in which move the sun and the moon, whom alone, of the gods, they say that they venerate. But as regards that which is straight: to this, also, there is a bound when it reaches its own place. For that which is earthly ceases entirely from motion, as soon as it has touched the earth. And every animal and vegetable makes an end of increasing when it has reached its limit. Therefore the stoppage of these things would be more properly the death of matter, than that endless death, which is, as it were, woven for it by them. But the motion which arises by a process of generation and corruption it is impossible to think of as in harmony with this hypothesis, for, according to them, matter is unbegotten. But if they ascribe to it the motion of alteration, as they term it, and that by which we suffer change by a quality affecting the sense, it is worthwhile to consider how they come to say this. For this seems to be the principal thing that they assert, since by matter it comes to pass, as they say, that manners are changed, and that vice arises in the soul. For in altering, it will always begin from the beginning; and, proceeding onwards, it will reach the middle, and thus will it attain unto the end. But when it has reached the end, it will not stand still, at least if alteration is its essence. But it will again, by the same route, return to the beginning, and from thence in like manner to the end; nor will it ever cease from doing this. As, for instance, if α and γ suffer alteration, and the middle is β, α by being changed, will arrive at β, and from thence will go on to γ. Again returning from the extreme γ to β, it will at some time or other arrive at α; and this goes on continuously. As in the change from black, the middle is dun, and the extreme, white. Again, in the contrary direction, from white to dun, and in like manner to black; and again from white the change begins, and goes the same round.

Chapter VIII.—Is Matter Wicked? Of God and Matter.

Is matter, in respect of alteration, an evil cause? It is thus proved that it is not more evil than good. For let the beginning of the change be from evil. Thus the change is from this to good through that which is indifferent. But let the alteration be from good. Again the beginning goes on through that which is indifferent. Whether the motion be to one extreme or to the other, the method is the same, and this is abundantly set forth. All motion has to do with quantity; but quality is the guide in virtue and vice. Now we know that these two are generically distinguished. But are God and matter alone principles, or does there remain anything else which is the mean between these two? For if there is nothing, these things remain unintermingled one with another. And it is well said that if the extremes are intermingled, there is a necessity for something intermediate to connect them. But if something else exists, it is necessary that that something be either body or incorporeal, and thus a third adventitious principle makes its appearance. First, therefore, if we suppose God and matter to be both entirely incorporeal, so that neither is in the other, except as the science of grammar is in the soul; to understand this of God and matter is absurd. But if, as in a vacuum, as some say, the vacuum is surrounded by this universe; the other, again, is without substance, for the substance of a vacuum is nothing. But if as accidents, first, indeed, this is impossible; for the thing that wants substance cannot be in any place; for substance is, as it were, the vehicle underlying the accident. But if both are bodies, it is necessary for both to be either heavy or light, or middle; or one heavy, and another light, or intermediate. If, then, both are heavy, it is plainly necessary that these should be the same, both among light things and those things which are of the middle sort; or if they alternate, the one will be altogether separate from the other. For that which is heavy has one place, and that which is middle another, and the light another. To one belongs the superior, to the other the inferior, and to the third the middle. Now in every spherical figure the inferior part is the middle; for from this to all the higher parts, even to the topmost superficies, the distance is every way equal, and, again, all heavy bodies are borne from all sides to it. Wherefore, also, it occurs to me to laugh when I hear that matter moving without order,—for this belongs to it by nature,—came to the region of God, or to light and brightness, and such-like. But if one be body, and the other incorporeal, first, indeed, that which is body is alone capable of motion. And then if they are not intermingled, each is separate from the other according to its proper nature. But if one be mixed up with the other, they will be either mind or soul or accident. For so only it happens that things incorporeal are mixed up with bodies.

Chapter IX.—The Ridiculous Fancies of the Manichæans About the Motion of Matter Towards God; God the Author of the Rebellion of Matter in the Manichæan Sense; The Longing of Matter for Light and Brightness Good; Divine Good None the Less for Being Communicated.

But in what manner, and from what cause, was matter brought to the region of God? For to it by nature belong the lower place and darkness, as they say; and the upper region and light are contrary to its nature. Wherefore there is then attributed to it a supernatural motion; and something of the same sort happens to it, as if a man were to throw a stone or a lump of earth upwards; in this way, the thing being raised a little by the force of the person throwing, when it has reached the upper regions, falls back again into the same place. Who, then, hath raised matter to the upper region? Of itself, indeed, and from itself, it would not be moved by that motion which belongs to it. It is necessary, then, that some force should be applied to it for it to be borne aloft, as with the stone and the lump of earth. But they leave nothing else to it but God. It is manifest, therefore, what follows from their argument. That God, according to them, by force and necessity, raised matter aloft to Himself. But if matter be evil, its desires are altogether evil. Now the desire of evil is evil, but the desire of good is altogether good. Since, then, matter has desired brightness and light, its desire is not a bad one; just as it is not bad for a man living in vice, afterwards to come to desire virtue. On the contrary, he is not guiltless who, being good, comes to desire what is evil. As if anyone should say that God desires the evils which are attaching to matter. For the good things of God are not to be so esteemed as great wealth and large estates, and a large quantity of gold, a lesser portion of which remain with the owner, if one effect a transfer of them to another. But if an image of these things must be formed in the mind, I think one would adduce as examples wisdom and the sciences. As, therefore, neither wisdom suffers diminution nor science, and he who is endowed with these experiences no loss if another be made partaker of them; so, in the same way, it is contrary to reason to think that God grudges matter the desire of what is good; if, indeed, with them we allow that it desires it.

Chapter X.—The Mythology Respecting the Gods; The Dogmas of the Manichæans Resemble This: the Homeric Allegory of the Battle of the Gods; Envy and Emulation Existing In God According to the Manichæan Opinion; These Vices are to Be Found in No Good Man, and are to Be Accounted Disgraceful.

Moreover, they far surpass the mythologists in fables, those, namely, who either make Coelus suffer mutilation, or idly tell of the plots laid for Saturn by his son, in order that that son might attain the sovereignty; or those again who make Saturn devour his sons and to have been cheated of his purpose by the image of a stone that was presented to him. For how are these things which they put forward dissimilar to those? When they speak openly of the war between God and matter, and say not these things either in a mythological sense, as Homer in the *Iliad*; when he makes Jupiter to rejoice in the strife and war of the gods with each other, thus obscurely signifying that the world is formed of unequal elements, fitted one into another, and either conquering or submitting to a conqueror. And this has been advanced by me, because I know that people of this sort, when they are at a loss for demonstration, bring together from all sides passages from poems, and seek from them a support for their own opinions. Which would not be the case with them if they had only read what they fell in with some reflection. But, when all evil is banished from the company of the gods, surely emulation and envy ought especially to have been got rid of. Yet these men leave these things with God, when they say that God formed designs against matter, because it felt a desire for good. But with which of those things which God possessed could He have wished to take vengeance on matter? In truth, I think it to be more accurate doctrine to say that God is of a simple nature, than what they advance. Nor, indeed, as in the other things, is the enunciation of this fancy easy. For neither is it possible to demonstrate it simply and with words merely, but with much instruction and labor. But we all know this, that anger and rage, and the desire of revenge upon matter, are passions in him who is so agitated. And of such a sort, indeed, as it could never happen to a good man to be harassed by them, much less then can it be that they are connected with the Absolute Good.

Chapter XI.—The Transmitted Virtue of the Manichæans; The Virtues of Matter Mixed with Equal or Less Amount of Evil.

To other things, therefore, our discourse has come round about again. For, because they say that God sent virtue into matter, it is worth our while to consider whether this virtue, so far as it pertains to good, in respect of God is less, or whether it is on equal terms with Him. For if it is less, what is the cause? For the things which are with God admit of no fellowship with matter. But good alone is the characteristic of God, and evil alone of matter. But if it is on equal terms with Him, what is the reason that He, as a king, issues His commands, and it involuntarily undertakes this labor? Moreover, with regard to matter, it shall be inquired whether, with respect to evil, the virtues are alike or less. For if they are less, they are altogether of less evil. By fellowship therefore with the good it is that they become so. For there being two evils, the less has plainly by its fellowship with the good attained to be what it is. But they leave nothing good around matter. Again, therefore, another question arises. For if some other virtue, in respect of evil, excels the matter which is prevailing, it becomes itself the presiding principle. For that which is more evil will hold the sway in its own dominion.

Chapter XII.—The Destruction of Evil by the Omission of Virtue Rejected; Because from It Arises No Diminution of Evil; Zeno's Opinion Discarded, that the World Will Be Burnt Up by Fire from the Sun.

But that God sent virtue into matter is asserted without any proof, and it altogether wants probability. Yet it is right that this should have its own explanation. The reason of this they assert, indeed, to be that there might be no more evil, but that all things should become good. It was necessary for virtue to be intermingled with evil, after the manner of the athletes, who, clasped in a firm embrace, overcome their adversaries, in order that, by conquering evil, it might make it to cease to exist. But I think it far more dignified and worthy of the excellence of God, at the first conception of things existent, to have abolished matter. But I think they could not allow this, because that something evil is found existing, which they call matter. But it is not any the more possible that things should cease to be such as they are, in order that one should admit that some things are changed into that which is worse. And it is necessary that there should be some perception of this, because these present things have in some manner or other suffered diminution, in order that we might have better hopes for the future. For well has it been answered to the opinion of Zeno of Citium, who thus argued that the world would be destroyed by fire: "Everything which has anything to burn will not cease from burning until it has consumed the whole; and the sun is a fire, and will it not burn what it has?" Whence he made out, as he imagined, that the universe would be destroyed by fire. But to him a facetious fellow is reported to have said, "But I indeed yesterday, and the year before, and a long time ago, have seen, and now in like manner do I see, that no injury has been experienced by the sun; and it is reasonable that this should happen in time and by degrees, so that we may believe that at some time or other the whole will be burnt up." And to the doctrine of Manichæus, although it rests upon no proof, I think that the same answer is apposite, namely, that there has been no diminution in the present condition of things, but what was before in the time of the first man, when brother killed brother, even now continues to be; the same wars, and more diverse desires. Now it would be reasonable that these things, if they did not altogether cease, should at least be diminished, if we are to imagine that they are at some time to cease. But while the same things come from them, what is our expectation of them for the future?

Chapter XIII.—Evil by No Means Found in the Stars and Constellations; All the Evils of Life Vain in the Manichæan Opinion, Which Bring on the Extinction of Life; Their Fancy Having Been Above Explained Concerning the Transportation of Souls from the Moon to the Sun.

But what things does he call evil? As for the sun and moon, indeed, there is nothing lacking; but with respect to the heavens and the stars, whether he says that there is some such thing, and what it is, it is right that we should next in order examine. But irregularity is according to them evil, and unordered motion, but these things are always the same, and in the same manner; nor will anyone have to blame any of the planets for venturing to delay at any time in the zodiac beyond the fixed period; nor again any of the fixed stars, as if it did not abide in the same seat and position, and did not by circumvolution revolve equally around the world, moving as it were one step backward in a hundred years. But on the earth, if he accuses the roughness of some spots, or if pilots are offended at the storms on the sea; first, indeed, as they think, these things have a share of good in them. For should nothing germinate upon earth, all the animals must presently perish. But this result will send on much of the virtue which is intermingled with matter to God, and there will be a necessity for many moons, to accommodate the great multitude that suddenly approaches. And the same language they hold with respect to the sea. For it is a piece of unlooked-for luck to perish, in order that those things which perish may pursue the road which leads most quickly to God. And the wars which are upon the earth, and the famines, and everything which tends to the destruction of life, are held in very great honor by them. For everything which is the cause of good is to be had in honor. But these things are the cause of good, because of the destruction which accompanies them, if they transmit to God the virtue which is separated from those who perish.

Chapter XIV.—Noxious Animals Worshipped by the Egyptians; Man by Arts an Evil-Doer; Lust and Injustice Corrected by Laws and Discipline; Contingent and Necessary Things in Which There is No Stain.

And, as it seems, we have been ignorant that the Egyptians rightly worship the crocodile and the lion and the wolf, because these animals being stronger than the others devour their prey, and entirely destroy it; the eagle also and the hawk, because they slaughter the weaker animals both in the air and upon the earth. But perhaps also, according to them, man is for this reason held in especial honor, because most of all, by his subtle inventions and arts, he is wont to subdue most of the animals. And lest he himself should have no portion in this good, he becomes the food of others. Again, therefore, those generations are, in their opinion, absurd, which from a small and common seed produce what is great; and it is much more becoming, as they think, that these should be destroyed by God, in order that the divine virtue may be quickly liberated from the troubles incident to living in this world. But what shall we say with respect to lust, and injustice, and things of this sort, Manichæus will ask. Surely against these things discipline and law come to the rescue. Discipline, indeed, using careful forethought that nothing of this sort may have place amongst men; but law inflicting punishment upon anyone who has been caught in the commission of anything unjust. But, then, why should it be imputed to the earth as a fault, if the husbandman has neglected to subdue it? because the sovereignty of God, which is according to right, suffers diminution, when some parts of it are productive of fruits, and others not so; or when it has happened that when the winds are sweeping, according to another cause, some derive benefit therefrom, whilst others against their will have to sustain injuries? Surely they must necessarily be ignorant of the character of the things that are contingent, and of those that are necessary. For they would not else thus account such things as prodigies.

Chapter XV.—The Lust and Desire of Sentient Things; Demons; Animals Sentient; So Also the Sun and the Moon and Stars; The Platonic Doctrine, Not the Christian.

Whence, then, come pleasure and desire? For these are the principal evils that they talk of and hate. Nor *does matter appear* to be anything else. That these things, indeed, only belong to animals which are endowed with sense, and that nothing else but that which has sense perceives desire and pleasure, is manifest. For what perception of pleasure and pain is there in a plant? What in the earth, water, or air? And the demons, if indeed they are living beings endowed with sense, for this reason, perhaps, are delighted with what has been instituted in regard to sacrifices, and take it ill when these are wanting to them; but nothing of this sort can be imagined with respect to God. Therefore those who say, "Why are animals affected by pleasure and pain?" should first make the complaint, "Why are these animals endowed with sense, or why do they stand in need of food?" For if animals were immortal, they would have been set free from corruption and increase; such as the sun and moon and stars, although they are endowed with sense. They are, however, beyond the power of these, and of such a complaint. But man, being able to perceive and to judge, and being potentially wise,—for he has the power to become so,—when he has received what is peculiar to himself, treads it under foot.

Chapter XVI.—Because Some are Wise, Nothing Prevents Others from Being So; Virtue is to Be Acquired by Diligence and Study; By a Sounder Philosophy Men are to Be Carried Onwards to the Good; The Common Study of Virtue Has by Christ Been Opened Up to All.

In general, it is worthwhile to inquire of these men, "Is it possible for no man to become good, or is it in the power of anyone?" For if no man is wise, what of Manichæus himself? I pass over the fact that he not only calls others good, but he also says that they are able to make others such. But if one individual is entirely good, what prevents all from becoming good? For what is possible for one is possible also for all. And by the means by which one has become virtuous, by the same all may become so, unless they assert that the larger share of this virtue is intercepted by such. Again, therefore, first, what necessity is there for labor in submitting to discipline (for even whilst sleeping we may become virtuous), or what cause is there for these men rousing their hearers to hopes of good? For even though wallowing in the mire with harlots, they can obtain their proper good. But if discipline, and better instruction and diligence in acquiring virtue, make a man to become virtuous, let all become so, and that oft-repeated phrase of theirs, the unordered motion of matter, is made void. But it would be much better for them to say that wisdom is an instrument given by God to man, in order that by bringing round by degrees to good that which arises to them, from the fact of their being endowed with sense, out of desire or pleasure, it might remove from them the absurdities that flow from them. For thus they themselves who profess to be teachers of virtue would be objects of emulation for their purpose, and for their mode of life, and there would be great hopes that one day evils will cease, when all men have become wise. And this it seems to me that Jesus took into consideration; and in order that husbandmen, carpenters, builders, and other artisans, might not be driven away from good, He convened a common council of them altogether, and by simple and easy conversations He both raised them to a sense of God, and brought them to desire what was good.

Chapter XVII.—The Manichæan Idea of Virtue in Matter Scouted; If One Virtue Has Been Created Immaterial, the Rest are Also Immaterial; Material Virtue an Exploded Notion.

Moreover, how do they say, did God send divine virtue into matter? For if it always was, and neither is God to be understood as existing prior to it, nor matter either, then again, according to Manichæus, there are three first principles. Perhaps also, a little further on, there will appear to be many more. But if it be adventitious, and something which has come into existence afterwards, how is it void of matter? And if they make it to be a part of God, first, indeed, by this conception, they assert that God is composite and corporeal. But this is absurd, and impossible. And if He fashioned it, and is without matter, I wonder that they have not considered, neither the man himself, nor his disciples, that if (as the orthodox say, the things that come next in order subsist while God remains) God created this virtue of His own free-will, how is it that He is not the author of all other things that are made without the necessity of any pre-existent matter? The consequences, in truth, of this opinion are evidently absurd; but what does follow is put down next in order. Was it, then, the nature of this virtue to diffuse itself into matter? If it was contrary to its nature, in what manner is it intermingled with it? But if this was in accordance with its nature, it was altogether surely and always with matter. But if this be so, how is it that they call matter evil, which, from the beginning, was intermingled with the divine virtue? In what manner, too, will it be destroyed, the divine virtue which was mingled with it at some time or other seceding to itself? For that it preserves safely what is good, and likely to be productive of some other good to those to whom it is present, is more reasonable than that it should bring destruction or some other evil upon them.

Chapter XVIII.—Dissolution and Inherence According to the Manichæans; This is Well Put, Ad Hominem, with Respect to Manes, Who is Himself in Matter.

This then is the wise assertion which is made by them—namely, that as we see that the body perishes when the soul is separated from it, so also, when virtue has left matter, that which is left, which is matter, will be dissolved and perish. First, indeed, they do not perceive that nothing existent can be destroyed into a nonexistent. For that which is non-existent does not exist. But when bodies are disintegrated, and experience a change, a dissolution of them takes place; so that a part of them goes to earth, a part to air, and a part to something else. Besides, they do not remember that their doctrine is, that matter is unordered motion. But that which moves of itself, and of which motion is the essence, and not a thing accidentally belonging to it—how is it reasonable to say that when virtue departs, that which was, even before virtue descended into it, should cease to be? Nor do they see the difference, that everybody which is devoid of soul is immoveable. For plants also have a vegetable soul. But motion itself, and yet unordered motion they assert to be the essence of matter. But it were better, that just as in a lyre which sounds out of tune, by the addition of harmony, everything is brought into concord; so the divine virtue when intermixed with that unordered motion, which, according to them, is matter, should add a certain order to it in the place of its innate disorder, and should always add it suitably to the divine time. For I ask, how was it that Manichæus himself became fitted to treat of these matters, and when at length did he enunciate them? For they allow that he himself was an admixture of matter, and of the virtue received into it. Whether therefore being so, he said these things in unordered motion, surely the opinion is faulty; or whether he said them by means of the divine virtue, the dogma is dubious and uncertain; for on the one side, that of the divine virtue, he participates in the truth; whilst on the side of unordered motion, he is a partaker in the other part, and changes to falsehood.

Chapter XIX.—The Second Virtue of the Manichæans Beset with the Former, and with New Absurdities; Virtue, Active and Passive, the Fashioner of Matter, and Concrete with It; Bodies Divided by Manichæus into Three Parts.

But if it had been said that divine virtue both hath adorned and does adorn matter, it would have been far more wisely said, and in a manner more conducing to conciliate faith in the doctrine and discourses of Manichæus. But God hath sent down another virtue. What has been already said with respect to the former virtue, may be equally said with respect to this, and all the absurdities which follow on the teaching about their first virtue, the same may be brought forward in the present case. But another, who will tolerate? For why did not God send someone virtue which could affect everything? If the human mind is so various towards all things, so that the same man is endowed with a knowledge of geometry, of astronomy, of the carpenter's art, and the like, is it then impossible for God to find one such virtue which should be sufficient for him in all respects, so as not to stand in need of a first and second? And why has one virtue the force rather of a creator, and another that of the patient and recipient, so as to be well fitted for admixture with matter. For I do not again see here the cause of good order, and of that excess which is contrary to it. If it was evil, it was not in the house of God. For since God is the only good, and matter the only evil, we must necessarily say that the other things are of a middle nature, and placed as it were in the middle. But there is found to be a different framer of those things which are of a middle nature, when they say that one cause is creative, and another admixed with matter? Perhaps, therefore, it is that primary antecedent cause which more recent writers speak of in the book περὶ τῶν διαφορῶν. But when the creative virtue took in hand the making of the world, then they say that there was separated from matter that which, even in the admixture, remained in its own virtue, and from this the sun and the moon had their beginning. But that which to a moderate and slight degree had contracted vice and evil, this formed the heaven and the constellations. Lastly came the rest encompassed within these, just as they might happen, which are admixtures of the divine virtue and of matter.

Chapter XX.—The Divine Virtue in the View of the Same Manichæus Corporeal and Divisible; The Divine Virtue Itself Matter Which Becomes Everything; This is Not Fitting.

I, indeed, besides all these things, wonder that they do not perceive that they are making the divine virtue to be corporeal, and dividing it, as it were, into parts. For why, as in the case of matter, is not the divine virtue also passible and divisible throughout, and from one of its parts the sun made, and from another the moon? For clearly this is what they assert to belong to the divine virtue; and this is what we said was the property of matter, which by itself is nothing, but when it has received form and qualities, everything is made which is divided and distinct. If, therefore, as from one subject, the divine virtue, only the sun and the moon have their beginning, and these things are different, why was anything else made? But if all things are made, what follows is manifest, that divine virtue is matter, and that, too, such as is made into forms. But if nothing else but the sun and moon are what was created by the divine virtue, then what is intermixed with all things is the sun and moon; and each of the stars is the sun and moon, and each individual animal of. those who live on land, and of fowls, and of creatures amphibious. But this, not even those who exhibit juggling tricks would admit, as, I think, is evident to everyone.

Chapter XXI.—Some Portions of the Virtue Have Good in Them, Others More Good; In the Sun and the Moon It is Incorrupt, in Other Things Depraved; An Improbable Opinion.

But if any one were to apply his mind to what follows, the road would not appear to be plain and straightforward, but more arduous even than that which has been passed. For they say that the sun and moon have contracted no stain from their admixture with matter. And now they cannot say how other things have become deteriorated contrary to their own proper nature. For if, when it was absolute and by itself, the divine virtue was so constituted that one portion of it was good, and another had a greater amount of goodness in it, according to the old tale of the centaurs, who as far as the breast were men, and in the lower part horses, which are both good animals, but the man is the better of the two; so also, in the divine virtue, it is to be understood that the one portion of it is the better and the more excellent, and the other will occupy the second and inferior place. And in the same way, with respect to matter, the one portion possesses, as it were, an excess of evil; while others again are different, and about that other the language will be different. For it is possible to conceive that from the beginning the sun and moon, by a more skillful and prudent judgment, chose for themselves the parts of matter that were less evil for the purposes of admixture, that they might remain in their own perfection and virtue; but in the lapse of time, when the evils lost their force and became old, they brought out so much of the excess in the good, while the rest of its parts fell away, not, indeed, without foresight, and yet not with the same foresight, did each object share according to its quantity in the evil that was in matter. But since, with respect to this virtue, nothing of a different kind is asserted by them, but it is to be understood throughout to be alike and of the same nature, their argument is improbable; because in the admixture part remains pure and incorrupt, while the other has contracted some share of evil.

Chapter XXII.—The Light of the Moon from the Sun; The Inconvenience of the Opinion that Souls are Received in It; The Two Deluges of the Greeks.

Now, they say that the sun and the moon having by degrees separated the divine virtue from matter, transmit it to God. But if they had only to a slight degree frequented the schools of the astronomers, it would not have happened to them to fall into these fancies, nor would they have been ignorant that the moon, which, according to the opinion of some, is itself without light, receives its light from the sun, and that its configurations are just in proportion to its distance from the sun, and that it is then full moon when it is distant from the sun one hundred and eighty degrees. It is in conjunction when it is in the same degree with the sun. Then, is it not wonderful how it comes to pass that there should be so many souls, and from such diverse creatures? For there is the soul of the world itself, and of the animals, of plants, of nymphs, and demons, and amongst these are distinguished by appearance those of fowls, of land animals, and animals amphibious; but in the moon one like body is always seen by us. And what of the continuity of this body? When the moon is half-full, it appears a semicircle, and when it is in its third quarter, the same again. How then, and with what figure, are they assumed into the moon? For if it be light as fire, it is probable that they would not only ascend as far as the moon, but even higher, continually; but if it be heavy, it would not be possible for them at all to reach the moon. And what is the reason that that which first arrives at the moon is not immediately transmitted to the sun, but waits for the full moon until the rest of the souls arrive? When then the moon, from having been full, decreases, where does the virtue remain during that time? Until the moon, which has been emptied of the former souls, just as a desolated city, shall receive again a fresh colony. For a treasure house should have been marked out in some part of the earth, or of the clouds, or in some other place, where the congregated souls might stand ready for emigration to the moon. But, again, a second question arises. What then is the cause that it is not full immediately? Or why does it again wait fifteen days? Nor is this less to be wondered at than that which has been said, that never within the memory of man has the moon become full after the fifteen days. Nay, not even—in the time of the deluge of Deucalion, nor in that of Phoroneus, when all things, so to speak, which were upon the face of the earth perished, and it happened that a great quantity of virtue was separated from matter. And, besides these things, one must consider the productiveness of generations, and their barrenness, and also the destruction of them; and since these things do not happen in order, neither ought the order of the full moon, nor the these of the waning moon, to be so carefully observed.

Chapter XXIII.—The Image of Matter in the Sun, After Which Man is Formed; Trifling Fancies; It is a Mere Fancy, Too, that Man Is Formed from Matter; Man is Either a Composite Being, or a Soul, or Mind and Understanding.

Neither is this to be regarded with slight attention. For if the divine virtue which is in matter be infinite, those things cannot diminish it which the sun and moon fashion. For that which remains from that finite thing which has been assumed is infinite. But if it is finite, it would be perceived by the senses in intervals proportionate to the amount of its virtue that had been subtracted from the world. But all things remain as they were. Now what understanding do these things not transcend in their incredibleness, when they assert that man was created and formed after the image of matter that is seen in the sun? For images are the forms of their archetypes. But if they include man's image in the sun, where is the exemplar after which his image is formed? For, indeed, they are not going to say that man is really man, or divine virtue; for this, indeed, they mix up with matter, and they say that the image is seen in the sun, which, as they think, was formed afterwards from the secretion of matter. Neither can they bring forward the creative cause of all things, for this they say was sent to preserve safety to the divine virtue; so that, in their opinion, this must be altogether ascribed to the sun; for this reason, doubtless, that it happens by his arrival and presence that the sun and moon are separated from matter.

Moreover, they assert that the image is seen in the star; but they say that matter fashioned man. In what manner, and by what means? For it is not possible that this should fashion him. For besides that, thus according to them, man is the empty form of an empty form, and having no real existence, it has not as yet been possible to conceive how man can be the product of matter. For the use of reason and sense belongs not to that matter which they assume. Now what, according to them, is man? Is he a mixture of soul and body? Or another thing, or that which is superior to the entire soul, the mind? But if he is mind, how can the more perfect and the better part be the product of that which is worse; or if he be soul (for this they say is divine virtue), how can they, when they have taken away from God the divine virtue, subject this to the creating workmanship of matter? But if they leave to him body alone, let them remember again that it is by itself immovable, and that they say that the essence of matter is motion. Neither do they think that anything of itself, and its own genius, is attracted to matter. Nor is it reasonable to lay it down, that what is composed of these things is the product of this. To think, indeed, that that which is fashioned by anyone is inferior to its fashioner seems to be beyond controversy. For thus the world is inferior to its Creator or Fashioner, and the works of art inferior to the artificer. If then man be the product of matter, he must surely be inferior to it. Now, men leave nothing inferior to matter; and it is not reasonable that the divine virtue should be commingled with matter, and with that which is inferior to it. But the things which they assert out of indulgence, as it were, and by way of dispensation, these they do not seem to understand. For what is the reason of their thinking that matter has bound the image of God to the substance of man? Or, why is not the image sufficient, as in a mirror, that man should appear? Or, as the sun himself is sufficient for the origination and destruction of all things that are made, hath he imitated an image in the work of their creation? With which of those things which he possessed? Was it with the divine virtue which was mingled with it, so that the divine virtue should have the office of an instrument in respect of matter? Is it by unordered motion that he will thus give matter a form? But all like things, in exquisite and accurate order, by imitating, attain their end. For they do not suppose that a house, or a ship, or any other product of art, is effected by disorder; nor a statue which art has fashioned to imitate man.

Chapter XXIV.—Christ is Mind, According to the Manichæans; What is He in the View of the Church? Incongruity in Their Idea of Christ; That He Suffered Only in Appearance, a Dream of the Manichæans; Nothing is Attributed to the Word by Way of Fiction.

Christ, too, they do not acknowledge; yet they speak of Christ, but they take some other element, and giving to the Word, designating His sacred person, some other signification than that in which it is rightly received, they say that He is mind. But if, when they speak of Him as that which is known, and that which knows, and wisdom as having the same meaning, they are found to agree with those things which the Church doctors say of Him, how comes it then that they reject all that is called ancient history? But let us see whether they make Him to be something adventitious and new, and which has come on from without, and by accident, as the opinion of some is. For they who hold this opinion say, as seems very plausible, that the seventh year, when the powers of perception became distinct, He made His entrance into the body. But if Christ be mind, as they imagine, then will He be both Christ and not Christ. For before that mind and sense entered, He was not. But if Christ, as they will have it, be mind, then into Him already existing does the mind make its entrance, and thus, again, according to their opinion, will it be mind. Christ, therefore, is and is not at the same time. But if, according to the more approved sect of them, mind is all things which are, since they assume matter to be not produced, and coeval so to speak with God, this first mind and matter they hold to be Christ; if, indeed, Christ be the mind, which is all things, and matter is one of those things which are, and is itself not produced.

They say it was by way of appearance, and in this manner, that the divine virtue in matter was affixed to the cross; and that He Himself did not undergo this punishment, since it was impossible that He should suffer this; which assertion Manichæus himself has taken in hand to teach in a book written upon the subject, that the divine virtue was enclosed in matter, and again departs from it. The mode of this they invent. That it should be said, indeed, in the doctrine of the Church, that He gave Himself up for the remission of sins, obtains credit from the vulgar, and appears likewise in the Greek histories, which say that some "surrendered themselves to death in order to ensure safety to their countrymen." And of this doctrine the Jewish history has an example, which prepares the son of Abraham as a sacrifice to God. But to subject Christ to His passion merely for the sake of display, betrays great ignorance, for the Word is God's representative, to teach and inform us of actual verities.

Chapter XXV.—The Manichæan Abstinence from Living Things Ridiculous; Their Madness in Abhorring Marriage; The Mythology of the Giants; Too Allegorical an Exposition.

They abstain also from living things. If, indeed, the reason of their abstinence were other than it is, it ought not to be too curiously investigated. But if they do so for this reason, that the divine virtue is more or less absent or present to them, this their meaning is ridiculous. For if plants be more material, how is it in accordance with reason to use that which is inferior for food and sustenance? Or, if there be more of the divine virtue in them, how are things of this sort useful as food, when the soul's faculty of nourishing and making increase is more corporeal? Now in that they abstain from marriage and the rites of Venus, fearing lest by the succession of the race the divine virtue should dwell more in matter, I wonder how in thinking so they allow of themselves? For if neither the providence of God suffices, both by generations and by those things which are always and in the same manner existent, to separate off the divine virtue from matter, what can the cunning and subtlety of Manichæus effect for that purpose? For assuredly by no giant's co-operation does assistance come to God, in order by the removal of generations to make the retreat of the divine virtue from matter quick and speedy. But what the poets say about the giants is manifestly a fable. For those who lay it down about these, bring forward such matters in allegories, by a species of fable hiding the majesty of their discourse; as, for instance, when the Jewish history relates that angels came down to hold intercourse with the daughters of men; for this saying signifies that the nutritive powers of the soul descended from heaven to earth. But the poets who say that they, when they had emerged in full armor from the earth, perished immediately after they stirred up rebellion against the gods, in order that they might insinuate the frail and quickly-perishing constitution of the body, adorn their poetry in this way for the sake of refreshing the soul by the strangeness of the occurrence. But these, understanding nothing of all this, wheresoever they can get hold of a paralogism from whatsoever quarter it comes, greedily seize on it as a God-send, and strive with all their arts to overturn truth by any means.

Chapter XXVI.—The Much-Talked-of Fire of the Manichæans; That Fire Matter Itself.

That fire, endowed indeed with the power of burning, yet possessing no light, which is outside the world, in what region has it place? For if it is in the world, why does the world hitherto continue safe? For if at some time or other it is to destroy it, by approaching it, now also it is conjoined with it. But if it be apart from it, as it were on high in its own region, what will hereafter happen to make it descend upon the world? Or in what way will it leave its own place, and by what necessity and violence? And what substance of fire can be conceived without fuel, and how can what is moist serve as fuel to it, unless what is rather physiologically said about this does not fall within the province of our present disquisition? But this is quite manifest from what has been said. For the fire existing outside the world is just that which they call matter, since the sun and the moon, being the purest of the pure, by their divine virtue, are separate and distinct from that fire, no part of them being left in it. This fire is matter itself, absolutely and *per se*, entirely removed from all admixture with the divine virtue. Wherefore when the world has been emptied of all the divine virtue which is opposed to it, and again a fire of this sort shall be left remaining, how then shall the fire either destroy anything, or be consumed by it? For, from that which is like, I do not see in what way corruption is to take place. For what matter will become when the divine virtue has been separated from it, this it was before that the divine virtue was commingled with it. If indeed matter is to perish when it is bereft of the divine virtue, why did it not perish before it came in contact with the divine virtue, or any creative energy? Was it in order that matter might successively perish, and do this *ad infinitum*? And what is the use of this? For that which had not place from the first volition, how shall this have place from one following? Or what reason is there for God to put off things which, not even in the case of a man, appears to be well? For as regards those who deliberate about what is impossible, this is said to happen to them, that they do not wish for that which is possible. But if nothing else, they speak of God transcending substance, and bring Him forward as some new material, and that not such as intelligent men always think to be joined with Him, but that which investigation discovers either to be not existing at all, or to be the extreme of all things, and which can with difficulty be conceived of by the human mind. For this fire, devoid of light, is it of more force than matter, which is to be left desolate by divine virtue, or is it of less? And if it is of less, how will it overcome that which is of more? But if it is of more, it will be able to bring it back to itself, being of the same nature; yet will it not destroy it, as neither does the Nile swallow up the streams that are divided off from it.

Elucidation.

If anything could be more dreary than the Manichæan heresy itself, it may be questioned whether it be not the various views that have been entertained concerning our author. I have often remarked the condensation of valuable information given by Dr. Murdock in his notes upon Mosheim, but he fails to get in the half that needs to be noted. He tells us that "Alexander of Lycopolis flourished probably about a.d. 350." He adds, "Fabricius supposes that he was first a Pagan and a Manichee, and afterwards a Catholic Christian. Cave is of the same opinion. Beausobre thinks he was a *mere pagan*. Lardner thinks he was a Gentile, but well acquainted with the Manichees and other Christians, and that he had *some knowledge* of the Old and New Testaments, to which he occasionally refers. *He speaks with respect of Christ* and the Christian philosophy, and appears to have been "a learned and candid man." Of an eminent Christian bishop, all this seems very puzzling; and I feel it a sort of duty to the youthful student to give the statements of the learned Lardner in an abridged form, with such references to the preceding pages as may serve in place of a series of elucidations.

According to this invaluable critic, the learned are not able to agree concerning Alexander. *Some think* he was a Christian, others believe that he was a heathen. Fabricius, who places him in the *fourth* century, holds to this latter opinion; all which agrees with our Cave. Photius makes him Archbishop of Nicopolis. Tillemont thinks he was a pagan philosopher, who wrote to persuade his friends to prefer "the doctrine of the churches" to that of Manes. Combefis, his editor, thinks him very ancient, because he appears to have learned the principles of this heresy from the immediate disciples of the heretic. Beausobre, the standard authority, is of like opinion, and Mosheim approves his reasoning.

Nothing in his work, according to Lardner, proves that our author wrote near the beginning of the fourth century, and he decides upon the middle of that century as his epoch.

Alexander gives a very honorable character to the genuine Christian philosophy, and asserts its adaptation to the common people, and, indeed, to all sorts of men. He certainly is not mute as to Christ. His tribute to the Savior is, if not affectionate, yet a just award to Him. By the "council of all together," he intends the College of the Apostles, made up of fishermen and publicans and tent-makers, in which he sees a design of the blessed Jesus to meet this class, and, in short, all classes. It is clear enough that Alexander has some knowledge of Christ, some knowledge of the received doctrine of the churches, or orthodox Christians; and he appears to blame the Manichees for not receiving the Scripture of the Old Testament.

     He argues against their absurd opinion that Christ was "Mind;" also that, though crucified, He did not suffer: and he affirms that it would be more reasonable to say, agreeably to the ecclesiastical doctrine, that "*He gave Himself for the remission of sins.*" He refers to the sacrifice of Isaac, and to the story of Cain and Abel; also to the mysterious subject of the angels and the daughters of men. Like an Alexandrian theologian, he expounds this, however, against the literal sense, as an allegory.

     My reader will be somewhat amused with the terse summing-up of Lardner: "I am rather inclined to think he was a Gentile...He was evidently a learned and rational man. His observations concerning the Christian philosophy deserve particular notice. To me this work of Alexander appears very curious."

Find this and other great works of the early Church Fathers at lighthousechristianpublishing.com.

Our Father who art in heaven, hallowed be thy name.
Thy kingdom come, Thy will be done, on earth as it is in heaven.
Give us this day our daily bread and forgive us our trespasses as we forgive those who trespass against us.
And lead us not into temptation, but deliver us from evil, for Thine is the kingdom, the power and the glory. Forever and ever.

Amen

Alexander of Lycopolis

Hail Mary full of grace, the Lord is with thee. Blessed art thou amongst women and blessed is the fruit of thy womb Jesus. Holy Mary mother of God, pray for us sinners, now and the hour of our death.

www.ingramcontent.com/pod-product-compliance
Lightning Source LLC
Chambersburg PA
CBHW052207070526
44585CB00017B/2103